What does the Bible say about what we will be like after we die?

Apostle Bill Amor

WHAT DOES THE BIBLE SAY ABOUT WHAT WE WILL BE LIKE AFTER WE DIE?
written by Bill Amor
1st Edition © 2025 by Bill Amor
ISBN: 979-8-9995696-5-3

Contents

CONTENTS

The Bible provides a multifaceted view of what we will be like after we die, emphasizing both an intermediate state and the ultimate resurrection of the body. In Apostle Bill Amor's new book, he explores these biblical teachings in depth, drawing from key scriptural passages and theological insights to offer clarity on this profound topic.

The Intermediate State: Conscious Existence with Christ

Apostle Bill Amor highlights that the Bible teaches believers will enter into a conscious, disembodied state immediately after death. This is often referred to as the "intermediate state," where the soul exists apart from the physical body but remains alive and in communion with Christ. For instance, Paul writes in **2 Corinthians 5:8**, "We are confident, I say, and would prefer to be away from the body and at home with the Lord." Similarly, in **Philippians 1:23**, Paul expresses his desire "to depart and be with Christ," which he describes as "better by far." These verses suggest that after death, believers are spiritually present with God while awaiting their bodily resurrection.

Resurrection of the Body: A Glorious Transformation

The ultimate hope for Christians lies not merely in a disembodied existence but in the resurrection of the body. Apostle Amor explains that this teaching is central to Paul's writings, particularly in **1 Corinthians 15**. Here, Paul compares our current bodies to seeds that are sown perishable but raised imperishable (1 Corinthians 15:42-44). The resurrected body will be transformed into a glorified state—imperishable, powerful, spiritual yet tangible—modeled after Jesus' resurrected body (Philippians 3:21). This transformation signifies victory over death through Christ's resurrection.

Judgment and Eternal Destiny

Apostle Amor also addresses what happens after death concerning judgment and eternal destiny. According to **Hebrews 9:27**, "It is appointed for man to die once, and after that comes judgment." Believers will stand before Christ at what is known as the "Judgment Seat of Christ" (2 Corinthians 5:10), where they will receive rewards based on their faithfulness during earthly life. Those who have rejected God face eternal separation from Him (Matthew 25:31-46). However, for believers, eternal life means dwelling with God forever in a renewed creation—a place described as free from pain, sorrow, or death (Revelation 21:4).

Metaphors Used by Paul

Amor delves into Paul's use of metaphors to describe life after death. For example:

- **The Tent vs. Building Metaphor** (2 Corinthians 5:1): Our earthly bodies are likened to temporary tents that will one day be replaced by eternal heavenly dwellings.

- **Clothing Imagery** (2 Corinthians 5:2-4): Paul speaks of being clothed with immortality so that we are not found "naked," symbolizing vulnerability without God's covering. These metaphors emphasize both the temporary nature of our current existence and the permanence of our future glorified state.

Hope for Believers

In his book, Apostle Amor underscores how these biblical truths provide hope and assurance for Christians facing mortality. The promise of being with Christ immediately after death offers comfort during grief. Moreover, the anticipation of bodily resurrection assures believers that death is not the end but a transition into eternal life.

By weaving together scriptural exegesis and theological reflection, Apostle Bill Amor's book serves as a comprehensive guide for understanding what happens after we die according to biblical teaching.

Introduction Commentary: Clothed or Naked Before Christ

The Bible is rich with imagery, symbolism, and profound truths that speak to the human condition and our ultimate destiny before God. Among these vivid depictions, the theme of being "clothed" or "naked" emerges as a powerful metaphor for spiritual readiness, vulnerability, and the state of one's soul in relation to Christ. From the Garden of Eden to the Book of Revelation, this motif weaves through Scripture, challenging us to consider how we will stand before Jesus—either clothed in righteousness or exposed in shame.

Consider two striking moments from the Gospels: John Mark fleeing naked after Jesus' arrest (Mark 14:51-52) and Peter casting off his outer garment to swim toward the risen Christ (John 21:7). These seemingly unrelated events are more than historical anecdotes; they serve as windows into deeper spiritual realities. John's naked flight symbolizes fear, abandonment, and human frailty in the face of divine purpose. In contrast, Peter's act of throwing off his clothes reflects urgency, devotion, and an unrestrained desire to be near his Savior. Both instances invite us to reflect on our own response when confronted with Jesus—will we run away in shame or draw near with boldness?

This theme crescendos in Revelation, where humanity is divided into two groups: those who are "naked" and those who are "clothed." The children of the lie—those who reject truth—are left exposed before God's judgment (Revelation 3:17). Their nakedness represents spiritual poverty and separation from God. Meanwhile, the children of truth are described as wearing robes washed white in the blood of the Lamb (Revelation 7:14). These robes signify purity, re-demption, and a life transformed by faith in Christ.

The contrast could not be starker. To be naked before Christ is to stand unprepared, vulnerable to judgment without the covering of His grace. To be clothed is to be wrapped in His righteousness—a gift freely given but requiring our acceptance through faith. This imagery compels us to ask ourselves: How will we meet Jesus? Will we approach Him clothed in garments cleansed by His sacrifice or exposed by our rejection of His truth?

As you journey through these pages, let this question resonate deeply within your heart. The stories of John, Mark's flight, Peter's leap into the water, and the ultimate vision of humanity standing before Christ are not just ancient narratives—they are mirrors reflecting our own spiritual reality. They challenge us to examine whether we have embraced the covering that only Jesus can provide.

This book invites you into a transformative exploration of what it means to be spiritually clothed or naked before God. It calls you to confront your fears, shed your pretenses, and embrace the cleansing power of Christ's sacrifice. For one day—whether through death or at His return—we will all stand before Him. May you find yourself clothed in robes washed white by His blood when that day comes.

Let this journey inspire you not only to prepare for that moment but also to live each day fully covered by His grace and truth.

The story of the rabbi or exorcist who attempted to cast out demons but was overpowered and humiliated is a reference to the biblical account in Acts 19:13-16. In this passage, the sons of Sceva, Jewish exorcists, tried to invoke the name of Jesus without truly knowing Him or having a relationship with Him. The demon they confronted responded, "Jesus I know, and Paul I know about, but who are you?" (Acts 19:15). The possessed man then attacked them violently, leaving them beaten and naked. This dramatic event serves as a powerful warning about the dangers of superficial religiosity and attempting to wield spiritual authority without genuine faith or connection to Christ.

In Apostle Bill Amor's new book, this narrative is used as a springboard to explore a profound spiritual truth: **those who rely on worldly religion or external appearances of piety will ultimately stand exposed before Jesus if they do not truly know Him.** This theme resonates deeply with Jesus' own warnings in Matthew 7:21-23, where He declares that not everyone who calls Him "Lord" will enter the kingdom of heaven. Instead, only those who do the will of His Father—those who have an authentic relationship with Him—will be recognized.

Introduction Commentary: A Call to Self-Examination

Imagine standing before the King of Kings at the end of your life. The weight of eternity hangs in the balance as you look into His eyes—eyes that pierce through every facade and see straight into your soul. Will He recognize you as one of His own? Or will He say those chilling words recorded in Matthew 7:23: "I never knew you; depart from Me"?

This sobering question lies at the heart of Apostle Bill Amor's exploration into what it means to truly belong to Christ. Drawing from Scripture, Amor paints a vivid picture of two groups who will stand before Jesus on that final day: **the children of truth**, clothed in robes washed white by the blood of the Lamb (Revelation 7:14), and **the children of lies**, left naked and ashamed because their outward religiosity masked an inner emptiness.

The story of the sons of Sceva serves as a cautionary

tale for all who place their trust in religious rituals, moral achievements, or intellectual knowledge rather than in a living relationship with Jesus Christ. These men invoked Jesus' name like a magic formula, hoping it would grant them power over evil spirits. But their lack of genuine faith was exposed when the demon mocked them and turned on them violently. Their humiliation—stripped naked and beaten—symbolizes what happens spiritually to those who rely on external forms of godliness while denying its true power (2 Timothy 3:5).

Amor challenges readers to examine their own hearts: Are you clothed in righteousness through faith in Christ? Or are you relying on your own efforts, traditions, or affiliations to secure your standing before God? The Bible makes it clear that only those whose names are written in the Lamb's Book of Life will enter His eternal kingdom (Revelation 20:15). For others, the worldly-religious who profess faith but lack true repentance, their works will be burned up like wood, hay, and stubble (1 Corinthians 3:12-15), leaving them spiritually naked before their Creator.

The Children of Truth vs. The Children of Lies

Apostle Amor contrasts these two groups using rich biblical imagery:

1. **The Children of Truth**
   These are believers whose lives have been transformed by God's grace through faith in Jesus Christ. They are described in Revelation 7:14 as wearing robes made white by being washed in the blood of

the Lamb—a metaphor for forgiveness and purifi-
cation through Christ's sacrifice on the cross. Their
clothing signifies their identity as redeemed saints
who belong fully to God.

Furthermore, these individuals walk in truth because they
abide in Christ (John 15:4-5). They bear fruit that reflects
their intimate relationship with Him—love, joy, peace, patience, kindness (Galatians 5:22-23)—and they persevere
even amidst trials because their hope is anchored in eternity.

2. **The Children of Lies**
   In stark contrast are those whom Jesus does not
   know—individuals who may outwardly appear religious but inwardly remain unregenerate. These are
   people like the Pharisees whom Jesus rebuked for
   being "whitewashed tombs" (Matthew 23:27)—clean
   on the outside but full of deadness within.

On judgment day, these individuals will find themselves
spiritually naked because they trusted in their own works
rather than Christ's finished work on Calvary. Like Adam
and Eve after their sin was exposed (Genesis 3:7), they will
experience shame and separation from God due to their
refusal to embrace His truth.

An Invitation for Reflection

As readers journey through this book's pages, Apostle Amor
invites them into a deeper understanding of what it means
to be known by Jesus—and how that knowledge trans-

forms every aspect of life. He urges believers not merely to profess faith but also to live it out authentically by walking humbly with God (Micah 6:8) and loving others sacrificially.

For those unsure where they stand spiritually—or for those caught up in empty religion—this book offers hope rooted firmly in Scripture's promises:

- "If we confess our sins," John writes reassuringly, "He is faithful and just to forgive us our sins and purify us from all unrighteousness" (1 John 1 :9).

Ultimately, Amor reminds us all: When we meet face-to-face with Jesus Christ, our eternal destiny hinges solely upon whether He knows us intimately. Will you be among children clothed with righteousness?

Here is a detailed outline of 12 chapters that would best cover Apostle Bill Amor's new book on what the Bible says about what we will be like after we die. Each chapter is designed to explore a specific aspect of biblical teaching on life after death, providing theological depth and practical insights for readers.

1. Introduction: The Mystery of Life After Death

This chapter sets the stage for the book by addressing humanity's universal questions about death and the afterlife. It introduces the biblical framework for understanding these topics and explains why they are central to Christian faith. Key themes include hope, resurrection, and eternal life.

2. What Happens Immediately After Death?

This chapter examines the "intermediate state," where believers' souls go immediately upon death. Scriptural references such as **2 Corinthians 5:8** ("to be away from the body and at home with the Lord") and **Philippians 1:23** ("to depart and be with Christ") are explored in detail. The chapter also addresses common misconceptions about soul sleep or unconsciousness.

3. The Nature of the Soul: Eternal or Temporary?

Here, Apostle Amor delves into what the Bible teaches about the nature of the soul. Drawing from passages like **Genesis 2:7** (the creation of man as a living being) and **Ecclesiastes 12:7** (the spirit returning to God), this chapter explores how humans are both physical and spiritual beings created for eternity.

4. Jesus' Teachings on Life After Death

This chapter focuses on Jesus' own words regarding life after death, including His parables (e.g., Lazarus and the rich man in **Luke 16:19-31**) and His promises to believers (e.g., "Today you will be with me in paradise" in **Luke 23:43**). It highlights how Jesus provides assurance of eternal life.

5. Paul's Vision of Resurrection Glory

Apostle Amor dedicates this chapter to Paul's teachings on bodily resurrection, particularly in **1 Corinthians 15**. Topics include the transformation from perishable to imperishable bodies, comparisons between Adam and Christ, and how resurrection is central to Christian hope.

6. The Resurrection Body: What Will We Be Like?

Building on Chapter 5, this section explores what Scripture reveals about our resurrected bodies. Passages like **Philippians 3:21** ("He will transform our lowly body to be like His glorious body") are analyzed alongside descriptions of Jesus' post-resurrection appearances as a model for believers.

7. Judgment After Death: Rewards or Separation

This chapter examines biblical teachings on judgment after death, including passages such as **Hebrews 9:27**, which states that people die once before facing judgment, and **2 Corinthians 5:10**, which speaks of believers appearing before Christ's judgment seat for rewards based on their earthly deeds.

8. Heaven as Our Eternal Home

Apostle Amor explores what heaven will be like according to Scripture, focusing on descriptions in passages like **Revelation 21-22**, which depict heaven as a place free from pain, sorrow, or death where God dwells with His people forever.

9. Hell: Eternal Separation from God

This chapter addresses one of the most challenging aspects of Christian theology—hell as eternal separation from God for those who reject Him. Key texts include Jesus' warnings in passages like **Matthew 25:41-46** ("Depart from me...into eternal fire") and discussions about God's justice and mercy.

10. Metaphors for Life After Death in Paul's Writings

Paul often uses metaphors to describe life after death, such as comparing earthly bodies to tents (**2 Corinthians 5:1**) or clothing (**2 Corinthians 5:4**) that will one day be replaced by something permanent and glorious. This chapter unpacks these metaphors to provide deeper understanding.

11. Living in Light of Eternity

This practical chapter encourages readers to live with an eternal perspective based on biblical truths about life after death. It discusses how hope in resurrection should influence daily decisions, relationships, suffering, and priorities.

12. Conclusion: Victory Over Death Through Christ

The final chapter ties together all earlier discussions by celebrating Christ's victory over sin and death through His resurrection (**1 Corinthians 15:54-57**) and its implications for believers today. It ends with an invitation for readers to embrace this hope personally.

By structuring Apostle Bill Amor's book around these chapters, readers can gain a comprehensive understanding of what Scripture teaches about life after death while being encouraged to live faithfully in anticipation of eternity.

Introduction: A Journey Beyond the Veil of Death

Death is one of life's greatest mysteries. It is a universal reality that every human being must face, yet it remains shrouded in uncertainty and fear for many. What happens when we die? Is there life beyond the grave? Will we recognize ourselves and others in the afterlife? These questions have echoed through the corridors of history, stirring the hearts and minds of countless individuals seeking answers.

For Christians, the Bible offers profound insights into these questions, providing hope and assurance about what lies beyond this earthly existence. The Scriptures do not leave us in the dark but instead illuminate a path that leads to understanding God's eternal plan for humanity. From Genesis to Revelation, the Bible reveals a consistent narrative about life after death—a narrative centered on God's redemptive work through Jesus Christ.

In this book, *What Does the Bible Say About What We Will Be Like After We Die?* I invite you to embark on a journey through Scripture to explore what God has revealed about our future existence. This is not merely an academic exercise or theological speculation; it is a deeply personal exploration of truths that impact how we live today and how we prepare for eternity.

The Bible speaks of two key stages in our post-death experience: an intermediate state where believers are present with Christ immediately after death, and the ultimate resurrection of our bodies at Christ's return. These teachings are not abstract doctrines but promises rooted in God's love and faithfulness. They assure us that death is not an end but a transition—a doorway into a new reality where we will experience fullness of life as God intended.

Throughout this book, we will examine key biblical passages that address life after death, including Paul's letters to the Corinthians and Thessalonians, Jesus' teachings in the Gospels, and John's vision in Revelation. We will also explore how these truths provide comfort during times of grief, inspire hope amidst uncertainty, and challenge us to live with eternity in mind.

As you read these pages, my prayer is that you will find clarity where there has been confusion, peace where there has been fear, and joy where there has been sorrow. The promise of eternal life is not just a distant hope—it is a present reality for those who trust in Christ. Together, let us uncover what awaits us beyond this life and marvel at the glorious future God has prepared for His children.

Welcome to this journey into eternity. May it deepen your faith, strengthen your hope, and fill your heart with anticipation for all that lies ahead.

In His Grace, Apostle Bill Amor

Heavenly Father, We come before You with hearts full of gratitude and praise. Thank You for the gift of life, for Your unending love, and for the grace that sustains us each day. Lord, we thank You for every reader who has opened this book. May their hearts be open to Your truth and their spirits enriched by the confidence that Jesus knows them intimately and loves them deeply.

Father, we acknowledge Your sovereignty over all things. We are reminded of Jesus' words in John 16:33: "In this world you will have trouble. But take heart! I have overcome the world." Thank You, Lord, for the assurance that no matter what trials or tribulations we face, we can rest in the victory of Christ. Through Him, we are more than conquerors.

We pray that as readers journey through these pages, they would experience a renewed sense of hope and peace in knowing that Jesus walks with them through every season of life. May they find strength in His promises and courage to face each day with faith.

Lord, bless each person who reads these words. May Your Spirit guide them into deeper understanding and intimacy with You. Let this book serve as a tool to draw them closer to Your heart and to remind them that they are never alone—Jesus has overcome the world on their behalf.

In Jesus' mighty name, we pray. Amen.

Chapter 1: Introduction: The Mystery of Life After Death

Death is one of the most profound mysteries of human existence. Across cultures, religions, and philosophies, humanity has wrestled with questions about what happens after we die. Is there life beyond the grave? If so, what will it be like? These are not merely abstract or academic inquiries; they strike at the very heart of our existence, shaping how we live, grieve, and hope. For Christians, these questions take on a unique significance because the Bible offers specific teachings about death and the afterlife that are central to the faith.

In this opening chapter, we will explore why understanding life after death is essential for every believer. We will examine how Scripture addresses these universal questions and provides a framework for hope rooted in God's promises. By setting the stage for this journey into biblical teaching on death and resurrection, this chapter invites readers to confront their fears, embrace their faith, and find assurance in the eternal truths revealed by God.

Humanity's Universal Questions About Death

From ancient civilizations to modern societies, humans have sought answers to life's ultimate question: What happens when we die? Archaeological evidence reveals that even prehistoric peoples buried their dead with care, often including items they believed would be needed in an afterlife. This suggests an innate awareness that death is not the end but a transition into something beyond.

Philosophers like Socrates pondered immortality; poets like Dante imagined vivid depictions of heaven and hell; scientists today study near-death experiences in search of empirical evidence for life after death. Yet despite millennia of inquiry, no human effort has fully unraveled this mystery. The Bible stands apart as a source of divine revelation on this subject. It does not leave us guessing but instead provides clear guidance about what lies ahead for those who trust in God.

The Bible acknowledges both the universality of death—"It is appointed for man to die once" (Hebrews 9:27)—and humanity's deep longing for eternity: "He has also set eternity in the human heart" (Ecclesiastes 3:11). These verses remind us that while death is inevitable, it is not natural or final. We were created for eternal communion with God—a truth that shapes everything Scripture teaches about life after death.

The Biblical Framework: Hope Beyond Death

At its core, Christianity is a religion of hope—a hope grounded in Jesus Christ's victory over sin and death through His resurrection. The apostle Paul declares in 1 Corinthians 15:17-19 that if Christ has not been raised from the dead, then Christian faith is futile. But because Christ *has* been raised as "the first fruits of those who have fallen asleep" (1 Corinthians 15:20), believers can face death with confidence rather than fear.

This hope extends beyond mere survival after physical death; it encompasses God's promise to restore all things through resurrection and renewal. As Paul writes in Romans 8:18-23:

"I consider that our present sufferings are not worth comparing with the glory that will be revealed in us... For we know that the whole creation has been groaning as in the pains of childbirth right up to the present time."

Here we see two key themes emerge: suffering and glory. While death brings pain and separation now, it also points forward to a future where God will wipe away every tear (Revelation 21:4) and make all things new (Revelation 21:5). This tension between present grief and future joy defines much of what Scripture teaches about life after death.

Why This Topic Matters

Why should Christians devote time to studying what happens after we die? First and foremost, understanding biblical teaching on this topic strengthens our faith by reminding us of God's sovereignty over life and death alike. In John 11:25-26 Jesus declares:

"I am the resurrection and the life. The one who believes in me will live even though they die; and whoever lives by believing in me will never die."

These words offer profound comfort during times of loss while also challenging us to live with an eternal perspective here on earth.

Secondarily—and perhaps more urgently—this topic matters because it equips believers to share their faith effectively with others who may be searching for answers about mortality or struggling with fear surrounding their own deaths or those they love dearly.

Finally—and most importantly—it matters because it glorifies God by pointing us back toward His ultimate plan for creation's redemption through Christ's work on Calvary's cross followed by His triumphant resurrection three days later!

Key Themes Introduced

As we embark on this journey together, throughout subsequent chapters exploring various aspects related specifically towards biblical teachings regarding posthumous existence, such as intermediate states versus final resurrections, alongside judgments plus rewards, etcetera, let us keep in the forefront of our minds the following thematic elements:

1. **Hope** - Rooted firmly within Gospel message proclaiming triumphs achieved via sacrificial atonement coupled alongside bodily resurrections.

2. **Resurrection** - Central doctrine affirming transformative nature awaiting faithful adherents modeled directly upon risen Savior Himself!

3. **Eternal Life** - Culminating reality wherein redeemed humanity dwells eternally amidst Creator enjoying full joys untainted sorrows forevermore!

By grounding ourselves firmly within scriptural truths concerning aforementioned topics readers shall gain deeper appreciation insights enabling them better navigate complexities surrounding mortal transitions ultimately leading towards everlasting destinations ordained divinely beforehand foundations world itself laid securely firmament above heavens below earth beneath oceans depths alike!

Chapter 2: What Happens Immediately After Death?

The question of what happens immediately after death has been a subject of deep theological reflection and debate throughout Christian history. For believers, the Bible provides clear and comforting answers about the state of the soul between physical death and the final resurrection. This period is often referred to as the "intermediate state." In this chapter, we will explore what Scripture teaches about this phase, focusing on key passages such as **2 Corinthians 5:8** and **Philippians 1:23**, while also addressing common misconceptions like "soul sleep" or unconsciousness.

The Intermediate State: A Conscious Presence with Christ

The Bible consistently affirms that for believers, physical death marks the beginning of a conscious existence in the presence of Christ. This teaching is perhaps most clearly articulated by Paul in **2 Corinthians 5:8**, where he writes, *"We are confident, I say, and would prefer to be away from the body and at home with the Lord."* Here, Paul contrasts life in our earthly bodies with being "at home" with Christ. The phrase "away from the body" implies that at death, there is a separation between the physical body and the soul or spirit. However, this separation does not result in unconsciousness or inactivity; rather, it leads to an immediate transition into God's presence.

Similarly, in **Philippians 1:23**, Paul expresses his personal longing for this intermediate state when he says, *"I desire to depart and be with Christ, which is better by far."* The word "depart" here refers to physical death, while "be with Christ" indicates a direct and conscious communion with Jesus after death. Paul's confidence that this state is "better by far" underscores its blessed nature for believers.

These passages provide assurance that upon death, Christians do not enter into a vague or shadowy existence but instead experience an intimate fellowship with their Savior.

Jesus' Teachings on Immediate Post-Death Existence

The teachings of Jesus further affirm that believers enter directly into God's presence after death. One of the most striking examples comes from Jesus' words to the repentant thief on the cross in **Luke 23:43**: *"Truly I tell you, today you will be with me in paradise."* Despite his impending physical death, Jesus assures the thief that he will join Him in paradise *that very day*. This statement leaves no room for ambiguity—there is no delay or unconscious waiting period between death and entering into fellowship with Christ.

Additionally, Jesus' parable of Lazarus and the rich man (**Luke 16:19-31**) provides insight into post-death consciousness. In this account, both Lazarus (the poor man) and the rich man are depicted as fully aware of their circumstances immediately after death. Lazarus finds comfort in Abraham's bosom (a metaphorical expression for being in God's care), while the rich man experiences torment. Though parabolic in nature, this story reinforces two key points: first, that individuals remain conscious after death; second, that their eternal destinies are determined immediately upon dying.

Addressing Misconceptions About Soul Sleep

One common misconception about what happens immediately after death is known as "soul sleep." This view suggests that when people die, their souls enter a state of unconsciousness until they are awakened at the final resurrection. Proponents of this idea often cite verses like **Ecclesiastes 9:5**, which states that *"the dead know nothing,"* or references to "sleep" as a metaphor for death (e.g., **John 11:11-14**).

However, careful examination reveals that these passages do not support soul sleep:

1. **Ecclesiastes 9:5** reflects Solomon's perspective on life "under the sun," emphasizing human limitations rather than providing theological commentary on life after death.

2. When Scripture uses "sleep" as a metaphor for death (e.g., John 11), it refers specifically to physical restfulness or bodily inactivity—not spiritual unconsciousness.

Moreover, numerous other biblical texts explicitly describe post-death consciousness for both believers and unbelievers (e.g., Luke 16; Revelation 6:9-11). These accounts make it clear that souls remain active and aware during the intermediate state.

The Nature of Being "With Christ"

What does it mean to be "with Christ" during this intermediate state? While Scripture does not provide exhaustive details about this experience, several truths can be discerned:

1. **Intimacy with God:** Believers enjoy direct communion with Christ without any barriers caused by sin or mortality.

2. **Rest from Earthly Struggles:** Revelation describes those who have died in faith as resting from their labors (**Revelation 14:13**). This rest includes freedom from pain, suffering, and sorrow.

3. **Anticipation of Resurrection:** While believers are spiritually present with Christ during this time, they await their ultimate hope—the resurrection of their bodies at Christ's return (**1 Thessalonians 4:16-17**).

This intermediate state serves as both a fulfillment of God's promise to His people and a prelude to even greater glory when heaven and earth are fully renewed.

Conclusion

In summary, Scripture teaches that immediately after physical death:

- Believers enter into a conscious existence where

they are spiritually present with Christ.

- This intermediate state is one of restfulness and joy but also anticipates future bodily resurrection.

- Misconceptions like soul sleep fail to align with biblical evidence regarding post-death consciousness.

For Christians facing mortality or grieving loved ones who have passed away in faith, these truths offer profound comfort. Death is not an end but rather a transition—a doorway leading directly into God's presence while awaiting His ultimate plan for creation's renewal.

Chapter 3: The Nature of the Soul: Eternal or Temporary?

In this chapter, Apostle Bill Amor examines one of the most profound questions in theology and human existence: the nature of the soul. Is the soul eternal, or is it temporary? Drawing from key biblical passages, he explores how Scripture reveals humanity's dual nature as both physical and spiritual beings, created in the image of God and destined for eternity.

The Creation of Humanity: A Living Soul

The foundation for understanding the nature of the soul begins with **Genesis 2:7**, which describes God's creation of humanity: "Then the Lord God formed a man from the dust of the ground and breathed into his nostrils the breath of life, and the man became a living being." This verse highlights two essential components of human existence:

1. **The Physical Body**: Formed from "the dust of the ground," humans are intrinsically connected to creation. Our physical bodies are finite and subject to decay (Genesis 3:19), emphasizing our earthly origin.

2. **The Breath of Life**: God's act of breathing life into Adam signifies more than mere biological function; it represents a divine impartation that animates humanity with a spiritual essence. The Hebrew word for "living being" (nephesh) is often translated as "soul,"

indicating that humans are not merely physical creatures but also possess an immaterial, spiritual dimension.

Apostle Amor explains that this duality—body and spirit—sets humans apart from other forms of creation. While animals are described as having "life" (Genesis 1:30), only humans are said to bear God's image (imago Dei) (Genesis 1:26-27). This unique status underscores humanity's eternal purpose and capacity for relationship with God.

The Soul's Eternal Nature

The Bible consistently portrays the soul as eternal, capable of existing beyond physical death. One key passage is **Ecclesiastes 12:7**, which states, "The dust returns to the ground it came from, and the spirit returns to God who gave it." Here, Solomon reflects on life's fleeting nature but affirms that while the body decays, the spirit endures and returns to its Creator.

Apostle Amor emphasizes that this verse aligns with other biblical teachings about life after death:

- **Matthew 10:28** warns believers not to fear those who can kill only the body but cannot destroy the soul. This distinction between body and soul implies that while physical death is inevitable, the soul persists.

- In **Luke 23:43**, Jesus assures the repentant thief on the cross, "Today you will be with me in paradise." This promise indicates an immediate continuation of conscious existence after death.

These passages affirm that human souls are not temporary entities tied solely to earthly existence but are designed for eternity.

The Image of God and Eternal Purpose

Apostle Amor delves deeper into what it means for humans to be created in God's image (Genesis 1:26-27). He explains that bearing God's image involves more than moral or intellectual capacities; it reflects an eternal aspect rooted in our spiritual nature. Just as God is eternal (Psalm 90:2), so too are human souls created with an eternal destiny.

This eternal purpose is further emphasized in passages like **John 3:16**, where Jesus declares that those who believe in Him will have "eternal life." The promise of eternity underscores God's intention for humanity—not annihilation or temporality but everlasting communion with Him.

Death as a Transition, Not an End

While Scripture teaches that physical death is a consequence of sin (Romans 6:23), it also presents death as a transition rather than an ultimate end. For believers, death marks entry into God's presence:

- Paul writes in **2 Corinthians 5:8**, "We are confi-dent...and would prefer to be away from the body and at home with the Lord."

- Similarly, in **Philippians 1:23**, Paul expresses his desire "to depart and be with Christ," which he describes as "better by far."

These verses suggest that while our bodies may perish temporarily, our souls remain alive and conscious in fellowship with God until they are reunited with glorified bodies at resurrection (1 Corinthians 15).

Temporary vs. Eternal Perspectives

Apostle Amor contrasts two perspectives on human existence:

1. **Temporary View**:

    - Some philosophies view human life as purely materialistic or finite.

    - Under this perspective, consciousness ceases at death because there is no immaterial soul.

    - However, such views conflict with biblical teachings about humanity's spiritual essence.

2. **Eternal View**:

    - The Bible affirms that humans were created

for eternity.

- Even though sin introduced mortality into creation (Genesis 3), redemption through Christ restores access to eternal life (Romans 6:23).

- This perspective provides hope beyond temporal suffering or loss.

Amor argues convincingly that embracing an eternal view aligns not only with Scripture but also with humanity's innate longing for meaning beyond this life—a longing Ecclesiastes describes as God having set "eternity in [our] hearts" (Ecclesiastes 3:11).

Implications for Believers

Understanding that our souls are eternal has profound implications:

1. **Hope Amid Mortality**:

- Believers can face death without fear because they know their souls will continue in God's presence.

2. **Accountability**:

- Recognizing our eternal destiny reminds us that earthly choices have lasting consequences (Hebrews 9:27).

3. Purposeful Living:

- Knowing we were created for eternity motivates us to live lives aligned with God's purposes rather than temporary pursuits.

Conclusion

In conclusion, Apostle Bill Amor affirms through careful biblical analysis that human souls are neither accidental nor temporary but divinely crafted for eternity. From Genesis' account of creation to New Testament promises about resurrection and eternal life, Scripture consistently reveals humanity's dual nature—physical yet spiritual—and ultimate destiny in relationship with God.

By understanding these truths about our souls' nature, believers can find comfort amid life's uncertainties and assurance about their future beyond this world.

Chapter 4: Jesus' Teachings on Life After Death

In this chapter, we delve into the teachings of Jesus Christ regarding life after death, focusing on His parables, direct statements, and promises to believers. Jesus' words provide profound insight into the nature of existence beyond the grave and offer assurance of eternal life for those who place their faith in Him. By examining key passages from the Gospels, we can better understand how Jesus addressed this critical subject during His earthly ministry.

The Parable of Lazarus and the Rich Man (Luke 16:19-31)

One of the most vivid accounts Jesus gives about life after death is found in the parable of Lazarus and the rich man in **Luke 16:19-31**. In this story, Jesus contrasts the earthly lives and eternal destinies of two individuals: a wealthy man who lived in luxury and a poor beggar named Lazarus who suffered greatly.

1. **The Earthly Contrast**:

    - The rich man enjoyed a life of comfort and abundance but showed no compassion for Lazarus, who lay at his gate covered in sores and longing for scraps from his table.

    - Lazarus represents those who suffer in this life but remain faithful to God.

2. **The Afterlife Realities**:

    - Upon death, Lazarus is carried by angels to "Abraham's side" (often interpreted as a place of comfort or paradise), while the rich man finds himself in Hades, a place of torment.

- This stark contrast underscores that one's eternal destiny is not determined by earthly wealth or status but by their relationship with God.

3. **Key Lessons**:

- The parable emphasizes that there is a fixed chasm between paradise and torment after death, making it impossible to cross from one side to the other (Luke 16:26).

- It also highlights the sufficiency of Scripture for guiding people toward repentance and salvation. When the rich man pleads for someone to warn his family, Abraham responds, "They have Moses and the Prophets; let them listen to them" (Luke 16:29).

This parable serves as both a warning about neglecting God's commands and an encouragement that faithfulness will be rewarded in eternity.

The Promise to the Thief on the Cross (Luke 23:43)

Another significant teaching on life after death comes from Jesus' interaction with one of the criminals crucified alongside Him. In **Luke 23:39-43**, one thief mocks Jesus, while the other acknowledges His innocence and asks to be remembered when He comes into His kingdom.

1. **Jesus' Assurance**:

- In response to this expression of faith, Jesus declares, "Truly I tell you, today you will be with me in paradise" (Luke 23:43).

- This statement provides several key insights:

  - Believers enter into a conscious state of being with Christ immediately upon death ("today").

  - The term "paradise" refers to a place of peace and fellowship with God.

  - Salvation is based on faith rather than works or merit—a truth demonstrated by this repentant thief who had no opportunity for good deeds yet received assurance of eternal life.

2. **Implications for Believers**:

   - This promise offers hope that even at life's final moments, sincere repentance can lead to salvation.

   - It also reinforces that eternal life begins immediately after physical death for those who trust in Christ.

Eternal Life Through Faith in Christ

Throughout His ministry, Jesus repeatedly emphasized that eternal life is available through faith in Him. Several key passages highlight this central theme:

1. **John 3:16-18**:

- In His conversation with Nicodemus, Jesus declares: "For God so loved the world that he gave his one and only Son, that whoever believes in him shall not perish but have eternal life."

- This verse encapsulates God's plan for salvation—eternal life is a gift offered freely through belief in Christ.

2. **John 11:25-26**:

- At Lazarus' tomb, Jesus proclaims: "I am the resurrection and the life. The one who believes in me will live, even though they die; and whoever lives by believing in me will never die."

- Here, Jesus asserts His authority over death itself and promises resurrection for all who believe in Him.

3. **John 14:1-3**:

- Before His crucifixion, Jesus comforts His disciples with these words: "Do not let your hearts be troubled... My Father's house has many rooms... I am going there to prepare a place for you."

- This passage assures believers that they have an eternal home prepared by Christ Himself.

Judgment and Eternal Separation

While much of Jesus' teaching focuses on assurance for believers, He also warns about judgment for those who reject God:

1. **Matthew 25:31-46**:

   - In this passage about the final judgment, Jesus describes separating people like sheep from goats based on their response to Him.

   - Those who cared for others are welcomed into eternal life ("the kingdom prepared since creation"), while those who ignored others' needs face eternal separation ("the eternal fire prepared for the devil").

2. **Mark 9:43-48**:

   - Jesus uses stark imagery to warn against sin leading to hell—a place described as where "the worm does not die" and "the fire is not quenched."

   - These warnings emphasize both God's justice and humanity's responsibility to respond appropriately during their earthly lives.

Assurance Through Christ's Resurrection

Finally, Apostle Bill Amor highlights how Jesus' own resurrection serves as proof of His teachings about life after death:

1. **Matthew 28; Luke 24; John 20-21**:

   - Following His crucifixion, Jesus rose bodily from the dead—appearing first to Mary Magdalene and later to His disciples.

- This event confirms that death has been defeated through Christ's victory (1 Corinthians 15:54-57).

2. **Revelation 1:17-18**:

- In John's vision on Patmos, Jesus declares: "I am the Living One; I was dead and now look—I am alive forever! And I hold the keys of death and Hades."

- These words affirm that Christ has ultimate authority over both physical death and spiritual destiny.

Conclusion

Jesus' teachings on life after death provide unparalleled clarity about what awaits humanity beyond this earthly existence. Through parables like Lazarus and promises such as "Today you will be with me in paradise," He assures believers that they will experience immediate fellowship with Him upon death—and ultimately share in bodily resurrection unto eternal glory.

By trusting fully in Christ's finished work on Calvary—and living faithfully according to His commands—believers can face mortality without fear but instead with confident hope rooted firmly within Scripture's timeless truths[123].

Chapter 5: Paul's Vision of Resurrection Glory

In this chapter, Apostle Bill Amor delves into one of the most profound and hope-filled passages in the New Testament: Paul's teaching on bodily resurrection as outlined in **1 Corinthians 15**. This chapter explores Paul's vision of resurrection glory, focusing on three key themes: the transformation from perishable to imperishable bodies, the theological comparison between Adam and Christ, and the centrality of resurrection to Christian hope.

The Transformation from Perishable to Imperishable Bodies

Paul's discussion in **1 Corinthians 15:35-58** addresses a fundamental question posed by skeptics: "How are the dead raised? With what kind of body will they come?" (1 Corinthians 15:35). In response, Paul uses vivid metaphors to describe the transformation that occurs during resurrection. He compares our current physical bodies to seeds that are sown into the ground. Just as a seed must die before it can grow into something new and glorious, so too must our earthly bodies undergo death before being raised in a glorified state.

Paul explains this transformation in terms of four contrasts:

1. **Perishable vs. Imperishable:**
   Our current bodies are subject to decay, illness, and death. However, at the resurrection, they will be raised imperishable—free from corruption or mortality (1 Corinthians 15:42).

2. **Dishonor vs. Glory:**

While our earthly existence is marked by frailty and limitations, our resurrected bodies will reflect God's glory and power (1 Corinthians 15:43).

3. **Weakness vs. Power:**
   Human weakness is evident in sickness and aging, but resurrection will bring strength and vitality beyond anything we can imagine (1 Corinthians 15:43).

4. **Natural vs. Spiritual:**
   Paul contrasts our current "natural" bodies—suited for life on earth—with "spiritual" bodies designed for eternal life with God (1 Corinthians 15:44). Importantly, "spiritual" does not mean immaterial; rather, it refers to a body fully empowered by God's Spirit.

Apostle Amor emphasizes that this transformation is modeled after Jesus' own resurrected body. As described in the Gospels, Jesus' post-resurrection appearances demonstrate both continuity and change—He could eat food and be touched (Luke 24:39-43), yet He also transcended physical limitations by appearing suddenly behind locked doors (John 20:19). Similarly, believers' resurrected bodies will retain their individuality while being gloriously transformed.

Adam vs. Christ: Theological Comparison

Another central theme in Paul's teaching is his comparison between Adam and Christ as representatives of two distinct humanities:

- **Adam as the First Man:**
  In **1 Corinthians 15:45-49**, Paul identifies Adam as the "first man," through whom sin entered the world

(Genesis 3). Because of Adam's disobedience, all humanity inherits mortality and corruption ("in Adam all die," 1 Corinthians 15:22).

- **Christ as the Last Adam:**
  In contrast, Jesus is described as the "last Adam" or "second man," who inaugurates a new creation through His obedience and resurrection (Romans 5:18-19). While Adam brought death to all his descendants, Christ brings life to all who belong to Him ("in Christ all will be made alive," 1 Corinthians 15:22).

Paul further elaborates on this contrast by describing two types of bodies associated with each figure:

- The first man (Adam) was made from dust and given a natural body suited for earthly life.

- The second man (Christ) came from heaven and possesses a spiritual body suited for eternal life.

Believers bear the image of Adam in their earthly existence but will bear the image of Christ in their resurrected state (1 Corinthians 15:49). Apostle Amor highlights how this theological framework underscores God's redemptive plan—to restore humanity through Christ's victory over sin and death.

Resurrection as Central to Christian Hope

For Paul—and for Christians throughout history—the doctrine of bodily resurrection is not an optional belief but a cornerstone of faith. Apostle Amor stresses that without resurrection, Christianity loses its meaning entirely.

Paul makes this point explicitly earlier in **1 Corinthians 15**:

- If there is no resurrection of the dead, then not even Christ has been raised.

- If Christ has not been raised, Christian preaching is useless, faith is futile, sins remain unforgiven, and believers have no hope beyond this life (1 Corinthians 15:12-19).

However, Paul triumphantly declares that Christ *has* been raised from the dead—the "first fruits" of those who have fallen asleep (1 Corinthians 15:20). This agricultural metaphor conveys that Jesus' resurrection is both a guarantee and a foretaste of what awaits all believers.

The chapter concludes with Paul's climactic vision of victory over death:

"When the perishable has been clothed with the imperishable...then the saying that is written will come true: 'Death has been swallowed up in victory.' Where, O death, is your victory? Where, O death, is your sting?" (1 Corinthians 15:54-55).

Apostle Amor reflects on how these verses encapsulate Christian hope—not merely survival after death but complete triumph over it through union with Christ.

Practical Implications for Believers

Finally, Apostle Amor considers how Paul's vision of resurrection glory shapes daily Christian living:

- It inspires perseverance amid suffering because present trials pale in comparison to future glory (Romans 8:18).

- It motivates holiness since believers are destined for eternal fellowship with God.

- It encourages steadfastness in ministry because labor for God's kingdom has eternal significance ("your labor in the Lord is not in vain," 1 Corinthians 15:58).

By grounding his readers firmly in Scripture while offering practical applications for today's challenges, Apostle Bill Amor provides a compelling exploration of Paul's teachings on bodily resurrection—a doctrine that continues to inspire hope across generations.

Chapter 6: The Resurrection Body: What Will We Be Like?

Building on the foundation laid in Chapter 5, this chapter delves into one of the most profound and hope-filled promises of Scripture: the resurrection body. The Bible teaches that believers will not remain as disembodied souls forever but will be clothed with a glorified, imperishable body at the resurrection. This transformation is central to Christian eschatology and provides a glimpse into the eternal future for those who are in Christ. By examining key biblical passages and reflecting on Jesus' post-resurrection appearances, we can begin to understand what our resurrected bodies will be like.

The Promise of Transformation

One of the clearest statements about the nature of our resurrection bodies comes from **Philippians 3:21**, where Paul writes:

"He will transform our lowly body to be like His glorious body, by the power that enables Him even to subject all things to Himself."

This verse reveals several important truths:

1. **Transformation**: Our current "lowly" or "humble" body subject to decay, weakness, and mortality—will undergo a radical change.

2. **Patterned After Christ's Glorious Body**: The resurrected body of Jesus serves as the prototype for
what believers can expect.

3. **Divine Power**: This transformation is accomplished
through God's omnipotent power, which is capable of
subduing all things under His authority.

Paul's teaching here assures us that our future bodies will
no longer bear the marks of sin and death but will instead
reflect the glory and perfection of Christ Himself.

Characteristics of the Resurrection Body

To understand what these transformed bodies will be like,
we turn to **1 Corinthians 15**, often referred to as "the resurrection chapter." In verses 35–49, Paul answers questions
about how the dead are raised and what kind of body they
will have. He uses analogies from nature and contrasts
between earthly and heavenly realities to describe four key
characteristics:

1. Imperishable

In **1 Corinthians 15:42**, Paul states:

*"So, it is with the resurrection of the dead. What is sown is
perishable; what is raised is imperishable."*

Our current bodies are subject to aging, illness, injury, and ultimately death. However, our resurrected bodies will no longer experience decay or deterioration. They will be eternal and incorruptible.

2. Glorious

Paul continues in **1 Corinthians 15:43**:

"It is sown in dishonor; it is raised in glory."

The term "dishonor" refers to the frailty and limitations of our earthly existence. In contrast, "glory" signifies radiance, beauty, and honor—qualities that reflect God's own majesty.

3. Powerful

Also in verse 43:

"It is sown in weakness; it is raised in power."

Our current physical state is marked by limitations—we grow tired, weak, and vulnerable. But our resurrected bodies will be endowed with strength and vitality beyond anything we can imagine.

4. Spiritual

Finally, Paul writes in **1 Corinthians 15:44**:

"It is sown a natural body; it is raised a spiritual body."

This does not mean that our resurrected bodies will be immaterial or ghost-like; rather, they will be fully suited for life in God's eternal kingdom—a realm governed by His Spirit.

Jesus' Resurrected Body as Our Model

The Gospels provide valuable insights into what our resurrection bodies might look like by describing Jesus' appearances after His resurrection. Since Philippians 3:21 tells us that our bodies will be conformed to His glorious body, these accounts serve as a template for understanding what awaits us.

Physical Yet Transcendent

Jesus' resurrected body was tangible—He invited Thomas to touch His wounds (John 20:27) and ate food with His disciples (Luke 24:42-43). Yet He also displayed abilities beyond normal human limitations:

- He appeared suddenly in locked rooms (John 20:19).

- He vanished from sight after breaking bread with two disciples (Luke 24:31).

- He ascended bodily into heaven (Acts 1:9).

These accounts suggest that while our resurrected bodies will retain physicality—they can interact with creation—they will also possess new capabilities suited for eternity.

Recognizable Yet Transformed

Jesus was recognizable after His resurrection but not immediately so:

- Mary Magdalene initially mistook Him for a gardener until He spoke her name (John 20:14-16).

- The disciples on the road to Emmaus did not recognize Him until He broke bread with them (Luke 24:30-31).

This indicates that while there may be continuity between our current appearance and our glorified state, there could also be differences reflecting our perfected nature.

Continuity and Discontinuity

Apostle Bill Amor emphasizes an important theological balance between continuity (what remains consistent) and discontinuity (what changes) when considering the resurrection body:

1. **Continuity**:

- Just as a seed grows into a plant while retaining its identity (1 Corinthians 15:37-38), so too will there be continuity between who we are now and who we become in eternity.

- Our personalities, memories, relationships—all redeemed aspects of who God created us to be—will carry over into eternity.

2. **Discontinuity**:

- The weaknesses associated with sin—the effects of aging, sickness, deformities—will no longer exist.

- Our new existence will transcend earthly limitations while still being grounded in physical reality.

Living in Light of Resurrection Hope

Understanding what Scripture teaches about our future glorified state has profound implications for how we live today:

- It encourages perseverance amid suffering (**Romans 8:18**) because present trials pale in comparison to future glory.

- It motivates holiness (**1 John 3:2-3**) since knowing we shall see Christ as He is inspires purity.

- It fosters hope (**1 Thessalonians 4:13**) because death does not have the final word for those who belong to Christ.

As Apostle Amor concludes this chapter, he reminds readers that these truths are not mere speculation but divinely revealed promises grounded in Christ's own victory over death—a victory shared by all who trust Him.

Chapter 7: Judgment After Death: Rewards or Separation

The Bible presents a clear and sobering teaching about judgment after death, emphasizing that every individual will face divine accountability for their lives. This chapter explores the biblical doctrines of judgment, focusing on the distinction between the judgment of believers and unbelievers, as well as the eternal consequences of these judgments. Drawing from key passages such as **Hebrews 9:27** and **2 Corinthians 5:10**, we will examine what Scripture reveals about this pivotal moment in human destiny.

The Certainty of Judgment

The Bible unequivocally teaches that judgment is an inevitable reality for all people. In **Hebrews 9:27**, it states, "It is appointed for man to die once, and after that comes judgment." This verse underscores two fundamental truths: first, that death is a universal experience, and second, that judgment follows immediately thereafter. There is no reincarnation or second chance after death; rather, each person's eternal destiny is determined by their response to God during their earthly life.

This certainty of judgment reflects God's justice and holiness. As the Creator and moral authority over all creation, God holds humanity accountable for how they have lived. The Apostle Paul reinforces this truth in **Romans 14:10-12**, writing, "For we will all stand before God's judgment seat... So then, each of us will give an account of ourselves to God." Every thought, word, action, and motive will be brought into the light of God's perfect standard.

The Judgment Seat of Christ (Believers' Judgment)

For believers in Jesus Christ—those who have placed their faith in Him for salvation—their sins have already been forgiven through His atoning sacrifice on the cross (Romans 8:1). However, this does not exempt them from standing before Christ's judgment seat to give an account of their lives. This event is often referred to as the "Judgment Seat of Christ" or the **Bema Seat**, based on Paul's description in **2 Corinthians 5:10**:

"For we must all appear before the judgment seat of Christ, so that each one may receive what is due for what he has done in the body, whether good or evil."

At this judgment, believers are not judged for their salvation—that issue was settled when they trusted in Christ—but rather for their works and faithfulness during their earthly lives. The purpose is to evaluate how they used their time, talents, resources, and opportunities to serve God and others.

Paul elaborates on this concept in **1 Corinthians 3:12-15**, where he uses the metaphor of a building being tested by fire:

"If anyone builds on this foundation using gold, silver, costly stones, wood, hay or straw, their work will be shown for what it is... If what has been built survives, the builder will receive a reward. If it is burned up, the builder will suffer loss but yet will be saved—even though only as one escap-

ing through the flames."

This passage highlights several key points:

1. Believers' works will be tested by fire to determine their quality.

2. Faithful service ("gold," "silver," "costly stones") results in eternal rewards.

3. Unfaithful or self-centered efforts ("wood," "hay," "straw") are burned away but do not affect salvation.

The rewards given at the Judgment Seat of Christ are often described as crowns or honors that reflect believers' faithfulness (e.g., **James 1:12**, **2 Timothy 4:8**, **1 Peter 5:4**). These rewards are not earned through human effort but are graciously bestowed by God as recognition of faithful stewardship.

The Great White Throne Judgment (Unbelievers' Judgment)

In contrast to believers' judgment at the Bema Seat stands the terrifying scene described in **Revelation 20:11-15**, known as the Great White Throne Judgment. This event pertains specifically to those who have rejected God's offer of salvation through Jesus Christ:

"Then I saw a great white throne and him who was seated on it... And I saw the dead, great and small, standing before the throne... Anyone whose name was not found written in the book of life was thrown into the lake of fire."

At this final judgment:

1. All unbelievers throughout history are resurrected to stand before God.

2. Their deeds are recorded in books that testify against them.

3. Because they rejected Christ's sacrifice for sin (John 3:18), they face eternal separation from God.

The imagery here conveys both God's justice and His sorrow over those who chose rebellion over reconciliation. While some may question how a loving God could allow such an outcome, Scripture emphasizes that He desires all people to repent and be saved (**2 Peter 3:9**) but does not force anyone against their free will.

Eternal Consequences

The outcomes of these judgments lead to two distinct eternal destinies:

1. **Eternal Life with God:** For believers who have trusted in Christ's redemptive work (John 3:16), eternity means dwelling with God forever in a renewed creation—a place free from pain, suffering, or death (**Revelation 21:1-4**).

2. **Eternal Separation from God:** For those who reject Christ's offer of salvation (Matthew 25:41), eternity involves separation from God's presence—a state described metaphorically as outer darkness or a lake of fire (**Matthew 25:46, Revelation 20:15**).

These realities underscore both God's holiness and His mercy—holiness because He cannot tolerate sin without justice being served; mercy because He provided a way for sinners to be reconciled through Jesus.

Living with Eternity in Mind

Apostle Bill Amor concludes this chapter by urging readers to live with eternity in mind. For believers:

- The promise of rewards should inspire faithful service out of love for Christ.

- The assurance of salvation should provide peace amidst life's uncertainties.

For those unsure about their relationship with God:

- The reality of coming judgment serves as an urgent call to repentance.

- God's invitation remains open until one's final breath (**John 6:37**).

Ultimately, understanding biblical teachings on judgment after death compels us toward gratitude for God's grace and motivates us toward holy living while there is still time.

Chapter 8: Heaven as Our Eternal Home

In this chapter, Apostle Bill Amor delves into the biblical portrayal of heaven as the eternal home for believers, drawing primarily from the vivid descriptions found in Revelation 21-22. These passages provide a glimpse into the ultimate fulfillment of God's redemptive plan—a place where His people will dwell with Him forever in perfect harmony, joy, and peace. By examining these scriptures and other related texts, Apostle Amor paints a picture of heaven that is both awe-inspiring and deeply comforting.

The New Heaven and New Earth

The Bible describes heaven not as an abstract or purely spiritual realm but as a tangible reality—a "new heaven and new earth" (Revelation 21:1). This phrase signifies the renewal and restoration of all creation. Apostle Amor emphasizes that this transformation is not merely about escaping the physical world but about God redeeming it. As Paul writes in Romans 8:21, creation itself will be "liberated from its bondage to decay" and brought into "the freedom and glory of the children of God."

This renewed creation will be free from all forms of corruption, suffering, and death. Revelation 21:4 declares, "He will wipe every tear from their eyes. There will be no more death or mourning or crying or pain, for the old order of things has passed away." This promise assures believers that heaven is a place where all brokenness is healed, all sorrow is erased, and life flourishes eternally.

The Dwelling Place of God with Humanity

One of the most profound aspects of heaven described in Scripture is that it will be the dwelling place of God with His people. Revelation 21:3 proclaims: "Look! God's dwelling place is now among the people, and He will dwell with them. They will be His people, and God Himself will be with them and be their God."

Apostle Amor explains that this marks the culmination of God's desire to have an intimate relationship with humanity—a theme woven throughout Scripture from Genesis to Revelation. In Eden, humanity walked with God; in heaven, this fellowship is fully restored on an even greater scale. No longer separated by sin or distance, believers will experience God's presence directly and eternally.

The Glory of Heaven

Revelation provides rich imagery to describe the glory of heaven. Apostle Amor highlights several key features:

1. **The New Jerusalem**
   Heaven is depicted as a magnificent city—the New Jerusalem—descending from God (Revelation 21:2). This city symbolizes both God's presence among His people and their eternal security within His care. Its dimensions are described as vast (Revelation 21:16), emphasizing its grandeur and capacity to accommodate all who belong to Christ.

2. **Radiance Beyond Compare**
   The city shines with "the glory of God" (Revelation

21:11), radiating light like a precious jewel. Unlike earthly cities that rely on artificial light sources such as lamps or sunlight, the New Jerusalem has no need for these because "the glory of God gives it light, and the Lamb is its lamp" (Revelation 21:23).

3. **Streets of Gold and Gates of Pearl**
   The streets are made of pure gold so transparent they appear like glass (Revelation 21:21), while each gate is fashioned from a single pearl (Revelation 21:21). These descriptions convey not only beauty but also perfection—everything in heaven reflects God's holiness.

4. **The River of Life**
   Flowing through the center of this heavenly city is "the river of the water of life," clear as crystal (Revelation 22:1). This river symbolizes eternal life flowing from God's throne—a reminder that He alone sustains life forever.

5. **The Tree of Life**
   On either side of this river stands "the tree of life," bearing twelve kinds of fruit each month for nourishment (Revelation 22:2). Its leaves are said to bring healing to nations—a powerful image signifying unity among all peoples under God's reign.

A Place Without Sin or Evil

Apostle Amor underscores that one defining characteristic of heaven is its complete absence of sin or evil. Revelation 21:27 states unequivocally that "nothing impure will ever enter it," nor anyone who does what is shameful or deceitful—only those whose names are written in the Lamb's

Book of Life may enter.

This purity ensures that heaven remains a place where righteousness dwells permanently (2 Peter 3:13). Believers can rest assured knowing they will never again face temptation or struggle against sin; instead, they will live in perfect holiness before their Creator.

Eternal Joy in Worship

Another central theme explored by Apostle Amor is worship in heaven. Revelation portrays countless multitudes gathered around God's throne singing praises to Him (Revelation 7:9-10). Worship becomes not just an activity but an expression flowing naturally outwards from hearts overwhelmed by gratitude for God's grace.

In addition to corporate worship scenes described throughout Revelation chapters four through seven—where angels join humans praising Christ—the book concludes emphasizing personal communion between individuals redeemed sharing direct access unhindered fellowship Creator Redeemer Savior alike!

In conclusion Apostle Bill Amor masterfully unpacks scriptural truths concerning eternal destiny awaiting faithful followers Jesus Christ!

Chapter 9: Hell: Eternal Separation from God

The doctrine of hell is one of the most sobering and challenging aspects of Christian theology. It confronts us with profound questions about God's justice, mercy, and the eternal destiny of those who reject Him. In this chapter, we will explore what the Bible teaches about hell as eternal separation from God, focusing on key scriptural texts, theological interpretations, and the implications for believers and non-believers alike.

The Biblical Basis for Hell

The concept of hell is firmly rooted in Scripture, with Jesus Himself providing some of the most vivid descriptions. One of the clearest passages is found in **Matthew 25:41-46**, where Jesus speaks about the final judgment:

"Then he will say to those on his left, 'Depart from me, you who are cursed, into the eternal fire prepared for the devil and his angels." (Matthew 25:41)

This passage highlights several key points:

1. **Hell as a Place of Separation**: Jesus' words "Depart from me" indicate that hell involves being cut off from God's presence.

2. **Eternal Nature**: The phrase "eternal fire" underscores that this separation is not temporary but everlasting.

3. **Prepared for Judgment**: Hell was originally created

as a place of punishment for Satan and his fallen angels but becomes the destination for those who reject God.

Other passages reinforce these themes:

- **Mark 9:43-48** describes hell as a place "where the worm does not die, and the fire is not quenched."

- **2 Thessalonians 1:9** states that those who do not know God or obey the gospel "will be punished with everlasting destruction and shut out from the presence of the Lord."

These verses collectively paint a picture of hell as both a physical reality (fire) and a spiritual condition (separation from God).

Theological Perspectives on Hell

1. Hell as Eternal Separation

One dominant view in Christian theology is that hell represents eternal separation from God's presence. This interpretation aligns with Paul's statement in **2 Thessalonians 1:9**, which emphasizes being "shut out" from God's glory. While God is omnipresent (Psalm 139:7-8), His relational presence—His love, grace, and fellowship—is absent in hell.

This separation is not arbitrary but stems from human choice. As C.S. Lewis famously wrote in *The Great Divorce*,

"There are only two kinds of people in the end: those who say to God, 'Thy will be done,' and those to whom God says, 'Thy will be done.'"

2. Hell as Justice

Apostle Bill Amor emphasizes that hell reflects God's perfect justice. Throughout Scripture, God is portrayed as holy and righteous (Isaiah 6:3; Psalm 89:14). Sin—rebellion against God's holiness—demands accountability (Romans 6:23). Hell serves as a demonstration of God's justice by holding individuals accountable for their rejection of Him.

In **Revelation 20:11-15,** John describes a scene where all humanity stands before God's throne to be judged according to their deeds. Those whose names are not found in the Book of Life are cast into "the lake of fire." This imagery reinforces that hell is not an arbitrary punishment, but a consequence tied to one's rejection of Christ.

3. Hell and Human Freedom

Another important theological perspective considers human freedom in relation to hell. Love requires free will; therefore, God does not coerce anyone into loving or following Him. Those who choose to reject God ultimately choose separation from Him—a decision that leads to hell.

As noted by theologian J.I. Packer:

"Scripture sees hell as self-chosen... Hell appears as God's

gesture of respect for human choice."

Common Misconceptions About Hell

Apostle Amor addresses several misconceptions about hell:

1. **Is Hell Literal Fire?** While many biblical descriptions use imagery like fire or darkness (e.g., Matthew 13:42; Jude 1:13), these may symbolize intense suffering rather than literal flames. The primary emphasis is on separation from God's presence rather than physical torment alone.

2. **Is Hell Temporary?** Some argue for annihilationism—the belief that souls cease to exist after judgment—or universalism—the belief that all will eventually be saved. However, traditional Christian teaching affirms that hell is eternal based on passages like Matthew 25:46 ("Then they will go away to eternal punishment").

3. **Does Everyone Go to Heaven Eventually?** While God's desire is for all people to come to repentance (2 Peter 3:9), Scripture consistently teaches that salvation requires faith in Christ (John 14:6). Those who reject this gift face eternal separation.

Balancing Justice and Mercy

One tension within discussions about hell lies between God's justice and His mercy:

- On one hand, God's holiness demands justice for sin.

- On the other hand, His love offers redemption through Christ's sacrifice.

Apostle Amor explains how these attributes converge at the cross:

"At Calvary, we see both God's wrath against sin poured out on Jesus and His mercy extended toward sinners."

Those who accept Christ's atoning work escape judgment (Romans 8:1), while those who reject it bear their own penalty.

Implications for Believers

Understanding the reality of hell has profound implications:

1. **Evangelism**: The urgency to share the gospel increases when we grasp what eternity apart from God entails.

2. **Gratitude**: Recognizing what believers have been saved from deepens our appreciation for Christ's sacrifice.

3. **Holiness**: Awareness of sin's consequences motivates us toward holy living.

Conclusion

Hell represents eternal separation from God—a sobering reality underscored by Jesus' teachings and affirmed throughout Scripture. While difficult to comprehend fully, it reflects both God's justice against sin and His respect for human freedom.

For believers, this doctrine serves as both a warning about rejecting Christ's offer of salvation and an encouragement to live faithfully while sharing His message with others.

Chapter 10: Metaphors for Life After Death in Paul's Writings

The Apostle Paul, one of the most influential figures in early Christianity, frequently used metaphors to describe complex theological concepts. Among these are his vivid and thought-provoking metaphors for life after death. These metaphors not only illustrate the temporary nature of our earthly existence but also point toward the eternal and glorious transformation awaiting believers. In this chapter, we will explore Paul's use of imagery such as tents, clothing, seeds, and buildings to convey profound truths about the Christian hope of resurrection and eternal life.

The Tent vs. Building Metaphor (2 Corinthians 5:1)

Paul begins 2 Corinthians 5 by contrasting our current physical bodies with a "tent" and our future resurrected bodies with a "building." He writes:

"For we know that if the earthly tent we live in is destroyed, we have a building from God, an eternal house in heaven, not built by human hands." (2 Corinthians 5:1)

This metaphor emphasizes the temporary and fragile nature of our earthly existence. A tent is a structure meant for short-term use—lightweight, portable, but ultimately impermanent. In contrast, a building represents permanence, stability, and strength. Paul assures believers that while their current bodies may be subject to decay and destruction (as tents eventually wear out), they will one day receive glorified bodies that are eternal and indestructible.

Paul's choice of this metaphor would have resonated deeply with his audience. Many early Christians were familiar with nomadic lifestyles or temporary dwellings like tents due to their socioeconomic conditions or cultural practices. By using this imagery, Paul connects their lived experiences to the hope of resurrection—a future where they will no longer inhabit frail "tents" but instead dwell securely in "buildings" provided by God.

Clothing Imagery: Being Clothed with Immortality (2 Corinthians 5:2-4)

In verses 2-4 of the same chapter, Paul shifts to another metaphor—that of clothing:

"Meanwhile we groan, longing to be clothed instead with our heavenly dwelling... so that what is mortal may be swallowed up by life." (2 Corinthians 5:2-4)

Here, Paul likens our current state to being inadequately dressed or even naked—a condition that symbolizes vulnerability and incompleteness. To be "clothed" with immortality represents receiving a new body at the resurrection that fully equips us for eternal life in God's presence.

This metaphor also reflects humanity's innate longing for restoration and wholeness. The "groaning" Paul describes captures both the physical suffering experienced in mortal bodies and the spiritual yearning for redemption. The promise of being clothed with immortality reassures believers that their struggles are temporary; they will one day experience complete renewal through Christ.

Paul's use of clothing imagery also echoes earlier biblical themes. For example:

- In Genesis 3:21, God provides garments for Adam and Eve after their fall into sin—a symbolic act pointing toward God's provision.

- Isaiah 61:10 speaks of being clothed with garments of salvation and righteousness.

By drawing on these rich biblical traditions, Paul reinforces the idea that God Himself will provide what is necessary for believers' ultimate transformation.

The Seed Metaphor: Sown Perishable, Raised Imperishable (1 Corinthians 15:35-44)

Another powerful metaphor used by Paul appears in his discussion of resurrection in 1 Corinthians 15. Here he compares death to planting a seed:

"What you sow does not come to life unless it dies... So, it will be with the resurrection of the dead. The body that is

sown is perishable; it is raised imperishable." (1 Corinthians 15:36-42)

This agricultural metaphor illustrates both continuity and transformation between our current bodies and our resurrected ones:

1. **Continuity**: Just as a plant grows from a seed without losing its identity as part of the same organism, so too will our resurrected bodies retain some connection to who we are now.

2. **Transformation**: However, just as a seed transforms into something far greater—a full-grown plant—our resurrected bodies will undergo radical change. They will no longer be subject to decay ("perishable") but will instead possess qualities suited for eternal life ("imperishable").

Paul uses this metaphor to address questions about how resurrection works practically—questions likely posed by skeptics or confused believers within Corinthian society. By grounding his explanation in everyday agricultural processes familiar to his audience, he makes an abstract theological concept accessible while emphasizing God's power over creation.

Groaning Creation: Anticipating Redemption (Romans 8:18-23)

In Romans 8:18-23, Paul extends his metaphoric language beyond individual believers to include all creation:

"We know that the whole creation has been groaning as in the pains of childbirth right up to the present time." (Romans 8:22)

Here he compares creation's suffering under sin's curse to labor pains preceding childbirth—a process marked by intense struggle but culminating in joy when new life emerges (John 16:21). This metaphor underscores two key points:

1. **Shared Longing**: Just as humans yearn for redemption through resurrection (v23), so too does creation await liberation from corruption.

2. **Certainty Amid Suffering**: Labor pains signify inevitable birth; likewise, present sufferings guarantee future glory because they are part of God's redemptive plan.

Through this imagery-rich passage combined with others explored earlier chapters readers gain deeper appreciation interconnectedness between humanity cosmos divine purposes fulfillment history itself.

Conclusion: Metaphors for Life After Death in Paul's Writings

In conclusion, Paul's use of metaphors to describe life after death serves as a powerful tool to communicate the profound transformation awaiting believers. By likening our earthly bodies to temporary tents and fragile clothing, Paul emphasizes the transient nature of our current existence. These vivid images contrast sharply with the permanence and glory of the resurrected body, which he describes as an eternal dwelling or being clothed with immortality. Through these metaphors, Paul not only illustrates the hope of resurrection but also reassures believers that their future state will be one of completeness, security, and divine fulfillment. This chapter has demonstrated how these symbolic expressions deepen our understanding of the Christian promise of life after death, offering both comfort and anticipation for what is to come.

Chapter 11: Living in Light of Eternity

The Bible's teachings about life after death are not meant to be abstract theological concepts or distant promises that have no bearing on our present lives. Instead, they are transformative truths designed to shape how we live every day. In this chapter, we will explore how the hope of resurrection and eternal life should influence our decisions, relationships, suffering, and priorities. Living with an eternal perspective is not just a lofty ideal—it is a practical way to align our lives with God's purposes and experience the fullness of His promises.

The Eternal Perspective: A Biblical Foundation

The Apostle Paul writes in **Colossians 3:1-2**, "Since, then, you have been raised with Christ, set your hearts on things above, where Christ is seated at the right hand of God. Set your minds on things above, not on earthly things." This passage calls believers to focus their thoughts and affections on eternal realities rather than being consumed by temporary concerns. Similarly, Jesus teaches in **Matthew 6:19-21** that we should store up treasures in heaven rather than on earth because "where your treasure is, there your heart will be also."

These verses remind us that our ultimate citizenship is in heaven (**Philippians 3:20**) and that our time on earth is fleeting compared to eternity. By keeping this eternal perspective at the forefront of our minds, we can make choices that reflect God's kingdom values rather than being swayed by worldly priorities.

How Hope in Resurrection Shapes Daily Decisions

Belief in the resurrection should profoundly impact how we approach daily decisions. Knowing that this life is not all there is frees us from living solely for immediate gratification or material success. Instead, it encourages us to invest in what has lasting value—our relationship with God and others.

Stewardship of Time and Resources

In light of eternity, how we use our time and resources takes on new significance. The psalmist prays in **Psalm 90:12**, "Teach us to number our days aright, that we may gain a heart of wisdom." Recognizing the brevity of life motivates us to use each day wisely for God's glory.

This means prioritizing activities that have eternal impact—such as sharing the gospel, serving others selflessly, and growing spiritually—over pursuits that are purely self-serving or transient. It also involves using financial resources generously to advance God's kingdom rather than hoarding wealth for personal comfort (**2 Corinthians 9:6-7**).

Making Choices That Reflect Eternal Values

When faced with moral or ethical dilemmas, an eternal perspective helps us choose what honors God even if it comes at a cost. For example:

- Choosing integrity over dishonesty at work because we know we will one day give an account before Christ (**2 Corinthians 5:10**).

- Forgiving others instead of harboring resentment because forgiveness reflects God's character and prepares us for heavenly relationships (**Ephesians 4:32**).

- Pursuing purity and holiness because these qualities align with who we are becoming in Christ (**1 Peter 1:15-16**).

Relationships Rooted in Eternity

Understanding eternity transforms how we view relationships. Every person we encounter has an eternal destiny—either with God or separated from Him—and this reality should shape how we interact with others.

Sharing the Gospel

One of the most loving things we can do for others is share the good news of Jesus Christ so they too can experience eternal life. Paul writes in **Romans 10:14**, "How can they believe in the one of whom they have not heard? And how can they hear without someone preaching to them?" Living with an eternal perspective compels us to prioritize evangelism as part of our daily lives.

This doesn't mean forcing conversations but being intentional about building relationships where spiritual discussions naturally arise. It also involves praying regularly for opportunities to share Christ's love and truth.

Loving Others Selflessly

Jesus commands us to love one another as He has loved us (**John 13:34-35**). When viewed through the lens of eternity:

- Acts of kindness take on greater meaning because they reflect God's love.

- Patience becomes easier when we remember that people are works-in-progress whom God is transforming.

- Reconciliation becomes urgent because broken relationships hinder both earthly peace and eternal joy.

Suffering Through the Lens of Eternity

Suffering is an inevitable part of life in a fallen world but hope in resurrection gives believers strength to endure trials with faith and perseverance.

Temporary Pain vs. Eternal Glory

Paul writes in **Romans 8:18**, "I consider that our present sufferings are not worth comparing with the glory that will be revealed in us." This perspective enables Christians to endure hardship knowing it serves a greater purpose—whether refining their character (**James 1:2-4**) or preparing them for future glory.

For example:

- Physical pain reminds us that these bodies are temporary but will one day be transformed into glorified bodies.

- Emotional struggles point us toward dependence on God as our ultimate source of comfort.

- Persecution for faith strengthens resolve by reminding believers they share in Christ's sufferings (**Philippians 1:29**).

Encouraging Others Amid Suffering

Living with an eternal mindset also equips believers to comfort others who are hurting by pointing them toward hope beyond their circumstances (**2 Corinthians 1:3-4**). Whether through prayerful support or practical help during difficult times, such acts demonstrate faith lived out tangibly.

Priorities Aligned With Eternity

Finally, living in light of eternity requires reevaluating what truly matters most:

1. **God First:** Cultivating intimacy with Him through prayerful dependence and Scripture meditation.

2. **People Second:** Investing deeply into family members' spiritual growth while extending grace outwardly toward neighbors/community.

3. **Mission Third:** Actively participating within church ministries aimed at advancing global discipleship efforts globally/local outreach initiatives locally alike!

Chapter 12: Conclusion: Victory Over Death Through Christ

The journey through the pages of this book has been one of discovery, reflection, and hope. We have explored the profound truths of Scripture regarding life after death, the intermediate state, the resurrection of the body, judgment, and eternal destiny. Now, as we conclude, it is fitting to focus on the ultimate triumph that makes all these promises possible: **Christ's victory over sin and death through His resurrection**. This victory is not only a cornerstone of Christian faith but also a source of unshakable hope for every believer.

The Triumph of Christ's Resurrection

The Apostle Paul declares in 1 Corinthians 15:54-57:

"When the perishable has been clothed with the imperishable, and the mortal with immortality, then the saying that is written will come true: 'Death has been swallowed up in victory.' Where, O death, is your victory? Where, O death, is your sting? The sting of death is sin, and the power of sin is the law. But thanks be to God! He gives us the victory through our Lord Jesus Christ."

This passage encapsulates the heart of Christian eschatology. Through His death on the cross and subsequent resurrection, Jesus conquered both sin and its ultimate consequence—death itself. Sin entered humanity through Adam (Romans 5:12), bringing separation from God and mortality into human experience. However, through Christ—the "last Adam" (1 Corinthians 15:45)—God provided a way to restore what was lost.

Jesus' resurrection was not merely a symbolic act; it was a historical event with cosmic implications. It demonstrated His power over death (Revelation 1:18) and served as a guarantee for believers that they too would share in this victory. As Paul writes in Romans 6:9-10:

"For we know that since Christ was raised from the dead, he cannot die again; death no longer has mastery over him. The death he died, he died to sin once for all; but the life he lives, he lives to God."

Because Christ defeated death once for all time, believers can face their own mortality without fear.

Implications for Believers Today

Assurance of Eternal Life

Christ's resurrection assures believers that physical death is not the end but rather a transition into eternal life with God. In John 11:25-26, Jesus declared:

"I am the resurrection and the life. The one who believes in me will live, even though they die; and whoever lives by believing in me will never die."

This promise provides comfort during times of grief and loss. For those who trust in Christ, there is certainty that they will be reunited with Him—and with other believers—in eternity.

Freedom from Fear

The fear of death often looms large in human experience. Yet Hebrews 2:14-15 reveals that Jesus came specifically to free humanity from this bondage:

"Since the children have flesh and blood, he too shared in their humanity so that by his death he might break the power of him who holds the power of death—that is, the devil—and free those who all their lives were held in slavery by their fear of death."

Through faith in Christ's victory over death, believers can live boldly and confidently without being paralyzed by fear.

Motivation for Holy Living

Paul concludes his discussion on resurrection in 1 Corinthians 15 with an exhortation to action:

"Therefore, my dear brothers and sisters, stand firm. Let nothing move you. Always give yourselves fully to the work of the Lord because you know that your labor in the Lord is not in vain" (1 Corinthians 15:58).

The knowledge that our earthly lives have eternal significance should inspire us to live faithfully for God's glory.

An Invitation to Embrace This Hope

As we close this book together, I want to extend an invitation—a personal call—to embrace this hope if you have not already done so. The victory over sin and death offered through Jesus Christ is available to everyone who believes (John 3:16). It does not depend on human effort or merit but solely on God's grace (Ephesians 2:8-9).

If you are reading these words today and feel uncertain about your eternal destiny or burdened by fear or doubt about what lies beyond this life, know that you do not need to carry those burdens alone any longer. Jesus invites you into a relationship with Him where you can find peace now and forevermore.

To accept this invitation:

1. Acknowledge your need for salvation due to sin.

2. Believe that Jesus died for your sins and rose again.

3. Confess Him as Lord over your life.

Romans 10:9 promises:

"If you declare with your mouth 'Jesus is Lord,' and believe in your heart that God raised him from the dead—you will be saved."

Final Words

In closing this chapter—and indeed this book—I pray that these reflections on Scripture have deepened your understanding of what awaits us after we die according to God's Word. More importantly, I hope they have filled your heart with joy at knowing **death has been defeated** through Christ's resurrection.

As we await His return when all things will be made new (Revelation 21:5), let us live each day anchored by this truth:

"He will wipe every tear from their eyes. There will be no more death or mourning or crying or pain—for the old order of things has passed away" (Revelation 21:4).

May you walk forward confidently into whatever lies ahead, knowing that because He lives—you too shall live forever.

Concluding Prayer of Thanks

Heavenly Father,

We come before You with hearts full of gratitude and praise. Thank You for the gift of Your Word, which illuminates the path before us and gives us hope for what lies beyond this life. Thank You for the assurance that through Jesus Christ, we are known, loved, and redeemed. We are humbled by the promise that even in death, we will be with You, and one day we will share in the glory of resurrection through Your Son.

Lord, we thank You for every reader who has journeyed through these pages. May they be enriched in their faith and confidence, knowing that Jesus knows them intimately and walks with them through every season of life. Strengthen their hearts to trust in Your promises, especially when trials and tribulations arise. As Jesus Himself said in John 16:33: "In this world you will have trouble. But take heart! I have overcome the world." May this truth bring peace to every soul and courage to face each day with unwavering hope.

Father, we ask that You bless each reader abundantly. Fill their lives with Your presence, guide them by Your Spirit, and remind them daily of the victory they have in Christ Jesus. May they live boldly as witnesses to Your love and grace until the day they stand before You in eternal joy.

In Jesus' mighty name we pray,
Amen.

About Apostle Bill Amor

Apostle Bill Amor's life is a testament to the power of faith, perseverance, and divine intervention. Diagnosed with autism as a child and considered high-functioning as an adult, Apostle Amor has faced challenges that would have broken many. Born into a world that often misunderstood him, young Bill struggled with feelings of isolation and inadequacy. Despite these challenges, he displayed remarkable determination. At the age of 12, he achieved a significant milestone by winning a reading competition—an accomplishment that filled him with pride and optimism.

However, this joy was short-lived when his mother tearfully shared devastating news from the doctor: he was not expected to live beyond the age of 28 to 32. This revelation shattered his world. Overwhelmed by fear and hopelessness, Bill sought solace in his best friend John Straw, only to discover that John had been taken away by his brother Andy. Feeling abandoned and consumed by anger, he fled into the woods near his home. It was there, amidst the trees and shadows of doubt, that he cried out to God in desperation. Bill's life changed forever on that fateful day. As he climbed a steep hill toward his neighbor's house, he encountered what can only be described as a divine vision: Jesus Christ Himself appeared before him at the top of the hill near a chain-link fence. The image was vivid—Jesus stood before him with pockmarks where His beard had been removed and glistening divots on His cheeks and chin. He did not resemble traditional depictions; instead, He appeared timeless yet distinct from modern trends.

This miraculous encounter marked the beginning of Apostle Amor's transformation. From a young boy who felt lost and unworthy, he grew into a man devoted to spreading God's message of love and repentance. Through trials and tribulations—including struggles with literacy—he found strength in faith and discovered his purpose as an apostle.

Apostle Amor's mission is clear: to guide others toward spiritual healing by sharing his testimony of divine grace. With humility born from hardship and wisdom gained through faith, he invites readers to embark on their own journeys toward repentance and renewal.